THE

Farm

WHISPERER

SECRETS TO PRESERVING FAMILIES
AND PERPETUATING FARMS

BY

DAVID SPECHT

WITH TANEIL SPECHT

Advising Generations publishes a variety of print and electronic formats and by print-on-demand. For bulk book orders contact us at (509) 318-0706 or visit us at AdvisingGenerations.com

--

Cover design and typesetting by: Joshua Kessie

--

Library of Congress Cataloging-in Publication Data:

Specht, David, 1978 — author.
The Farm Whisperer: Secrets to Preserving Families and Perpetuating Farms / David Specht..

Pages 144 cm

Includes index.

ISBN: 978-0-9965979-0-6 (paperback)

1. Family-owned farms—Succession/Management
2. Professional Advising—Transition Planning

First Edition

TO MY WIFE TANEIL AND MY CHILDREN
MAKALEY, DAMON, REICHERT, JHETT AND
LIBERTY. YOUR SUPPORT AND UNCONDITIONAL
LOVE INSPIRES ME.

TO MY PARENTS, CLIFF AND CHRIS SPECHT
AND MY SIBLINGS, AMIE, D.J. AND JACLYN.
YOU ALWAYS TOLD ME I COULD ACCOMPLISH
ANYTHING AND I BELIEVED YOU.

AND TO JIM ABEL FOR MAKING IT POSSIBLE
TO TEACH THE NEXT GENERATION OF FAMILY
BUSINESS LEADERS AT THE UNIVERSITY OF
NEBRASKA. AND FINALLY, TO ALL OF THE
FAMILIES THAT I HAVE CONSULTED WITH. I
HONOR THE TRUST YOU HAVE PUT IN ME AND
THIS BOOK IS DEDICATED TO YOU.

CONTENTS

SPECHT

PREFACE

T he path that I have chosen in life has never been the easy way. Whether it was choosing to walk on to the basketball team in college, spend two years in South America as a missionary or get married and start a family before graduating college. I've always pursued opportunities that people questioned as unattainable or just plain hard.

I became interested in working with multi-generational family businesses when I was finishing my graduate degree in Tax and Financial Planning at San Diego State University. I needed one elective class to finish my degree. I decided to take a course in Family Business Management from Carmen Bianchi and my perspective on what I wanted to do with my professional life changed forever.

This course blended the financial and the non-financial issues that families face and gave me the idea that I could make a job out of helping families to stay families, while perpetuating their business legacies.

A significant part of my work has been in agriculture. Family farms and ranches are a special part of what makes America great. Agriculture is all about people working, sacrificing, struggling and also being successful TOGETHER. I observe families that love building great operations, teaching their kids the value of work and responsibility. I also see families torn apart due to a lack of communication and no coordinated plan for ownership or management.

I often think to myself, how can I help prevent families from this pain? This question drives me to consult, write and speak all over the country. It drives me to create the Inspired Questions—For Farmers Mobile App, the GenerationalBusiness360 process and now to write, The Farm Whisperer.

This feels like a calling for me because every family is a unique puzzle. With each family that I touch, I realize that I have an opportunity to influence them individually, as a family, their employees and the community where their business is located.

This work is a labor of love for me. I hope that something in this book gives you the desire to make choices and plans to Preserve Your Family and Perpetuate Your Legacy.

INTRODUCTION

The Farm Whisperer is a derivative of a nickname that was given to me by a writer in Omaha, Nebraska. To me The Farm Whisperer isn't about me, it's about a process that each of us can go through to ask the right questions, pursue the appropriate conversations and implement the best solutions for you personally and for your farm.

The Farm Whisperer is a compilation of articles and stories that are meant to assist farm families and the professionals that advise them. The book is laid out in a way that encourages you to think introspectively about the "Inspired Question" at the end of each chapter and then to allow you and then reflect and create an action plan for how you will implement solutions based on what you have learned.

The purpose for this book is to lead you to an intentional planning process that ultimately preserves your family relationships and perpetuates your farm legacy.

1

THE POWER OF AN INSPIRED QUESTION

Inspired Questions lead to Inspired Answers.

—DAVID A. BEDNAR

I'm 23. I'm still in college. And I don't really know how I'm going to provide for my family. What happens when she comes to me with questions and I don't have the answers?

I had been a father for only a matter of months, and when I looked into the eyes of my newborn girl as I held her each night, anxiety filled my body. Worry robbed me of sleep, concerns about choosing the right career path and buying groceries now, raising a child in an increasingly turbulent world and finishing a term paper compounded and built until they eclipsed the moments of joy that I should have been experiencing with my wife and little girl. After weeks of worry, I finally decided to confide in my college professor, David A. Bednar. I had an interview scheduled with him so I built up some courage and told him what I was feeling.

"David," he said, he was one of the few people who called me by my full given name, "you don't have to worry about not having all the right answers, just make sure you have the right questions." In that moment I didn't quite understand that advice, but I have come to not only appreciate it, but increasingly I try to live and teach others about the power of an inspired question.

This was not the kind of straightforward answer that I had hoped for, but it provided me a framework to build off of. Throughout the years I have worked on developing questions that I could ask my little girl that would allow us to have a meaningful conversation and develop our father-daughter relationship.

As I was working on this in my personal life it became evident that asking, "inspired questions" was also very valuable in other parts of my life. I translated this skill with great intentionality when I began working with farmers and business owners that I was consulting with about management and ownership succession. I quickly learned that A-type personalities and independent minded people didn't want to be told what to do. I could bring them a solution and tell them all the benefits, but if it wasn't their idea, they wouldn't implement. I decided to spend the bulk of my time preparing questions that would lead the farmer or business owner to their own conclusions and then I would help them see those ideas to fruition. It was magical and very effective!

I no longer had to worry about canvassing the pros and cons of every possible solution or pretend to be the smartest person in the room. I just had to focus on developing questions that would bring clarity to the family as they discovered the solutions that worked best for their group of interests and personalities, and then help lead the team of professionals to turn these ideas into tangible reality.

At the end of each chapter in "The Farm Whisperer" you will be given an Inspired Question to reflect on. This exercise is meant to make each chapter meaningful, actionable and interactive with your farm family. Each chapter should be applied to your own situation and you should write down your reflections and the things that you will commit to work on to increase the likelihood of the continuity of your farm.

Inspired Questions require thoughtful reflection, brutal honesty and most importantly, a sincere desire to achieve solutions that bring out the potential greatness in the rising generation while securing the rewards due to those owners and leaders who have given so much of their lives building the farm.

Grandpa's Old Kubota

2

LIFE LESSONS FROM THE TRACTOR SEAT

*Opportunity is missed by most people because
it is dressed in overalls and looks like work.*

—THOMAS A. EDISON

The incessant throb and hum of the engine, the pulling and churning of the implement interrupted only by the beeps of the monitoring equipment or the crackle of the radio can become mind numbing. It was for me until I opened my eyes and mind to the life lessons unfolding all around me. During harvest, tractor drivers are blessed with LOTS of time to think, especially with GPS and the other comforts that modern equipment now provide. While working fields, preparing them for planting winter wheat or next year's potatoes, it dawned on me that I was in a front row seat to some prime education on living well.

WHEN IT'S POSSIBLE, TURN INTO SHORT ROWS.

As a tractor driver there are a few different ways to move through the field. Depending on the implement you are pulling behind you, the room you have on the outside passes and the shape of the field, you need to determine the best course of action. My farming scenario—120 acre field laid out in a circle, I was pulling a Turbo-Chisel® and packers.

As a rookie tractor driver I became frustrated over the way that I was required to turn the tractor, from short rows into longer rows. The turns were too sharp, they left the ends a mess and there were "skips" in the field because of the way I was turning. A more experienced tractor driver gave me some really simple advice. "When you can, turn into short rows." This may seem intuitive to those that are experienced tractor drivers, but to me, it was a revelation.

Life is full of choices and advice from more experienced people can help us to avoid some of the pains. Making decisions in our life based on good counsel from experienced mentors helps to avoid those actions that unintentionally make life harder or more complicated. Simple, basic truths that too many of us fail to follow. For example, when was the last time you had three nights in a row of adequate sleep? What did you last spend money on when you were under stress? Neglecting sleep or becoming involved in drug or alcohol abuse can complicate your life and frustrate you in the accomplishment of your overall objectives for your life.

ALWAYS TRUST YOUR INTERNAL COMPASS
REGARDING EXTERIOR BOUNDARIES

GPS technology has revolutionized the precision with which farming is now accomplished. In my experience GPS is still only as effective as the person who sets up the field in the system. Example: While tilling the outside rows of a field I noticed that if I relied solely on my GPS that I would be farming in the weeds and be outside of my desired boundaries.

In life, popular culture and social media are doing their best to determine where our boundaries should be. If we choose to allow the technologies and popular media outlets of the day to determine what we believe and how we will act, we may find ourselves "farming in the weeds" and not accomplishing what our long-term goal is. When it comes to boundaries, whether in our tractors or in our lives, we should pay close attention to our internal compass and adjust the technologies in our life accordingly to assist us in the accomplishments of our objective.

WHEN THE PULLING GETS TOUGH, DON'T QUIT

While preparing a new field for potatoes the farmer decided that it would be best to use a Paratill® behind the tractor and then follow that up with a packer. The Paratill® was used to go deep into the soil to break up the hardpan layer that had formed over the years. At times, pulling was hard, but as I shifted down to a lower gear, slowed my pace and sometimes adjusted the depth of the Paratill®, the tractor was able to continue through the field and accomplish the goal.

In life, sometimes we have seasons of "hard pulling." It may be necessary to slow down and even adjust our depth to be able to make it through the hard times. The key is to not give up, but to keep going, even if you have to slow your pace or adjust the amount of things you are trying to accomplish. It may not always lead to the ideal outcome, but it will be better than giving up when the pulling gets tough.

DON'T OVERLOOK DAILY MAINTENANCE

While tractors are powerful and seemingly indestructible at times, they need consistent maintenance. Daily monitoring of the oil levels, hydraulic fluids and making sure your implements get proper amount of lubrication is key to ongoing functionality.

Many times in life we get going so fast that we neglect some of the daily maintenance items in our life that are needed to keep us healthy, alert and functioning properly. Taking time for proper rest and exercise, eating well and paying attention to our social and spiritual needs individually, and as a family, will go a long way in avoiding major breakdowns.

AT TIMES ALL YOU CAN DO IS FOCUS
ON THE ROW YOU ARE WORKING ON

When working at night or before dawn it can be hard to see, especially when you are making turns in the field. Using GPS and focusing on what you can see is often the best you can do. As the day breaks and the sun begins to rise, your perspective broadens and you can see how the work you are accomplishing fits in relation to the whole field. Sometimes in life all you can do is focus on your row and do the best you can. Time alone will bring perspective and help you see your life in the broader context.

Life events sometimes are so consuming that we need all of our energy and focus just to get through them. This may come in the form of losing a loved one, an illness, a divorce or some other setback in life. When going through these things we may not be able to see the big picture of how the event fits in our overall life, but as time passes our perspective broadens and our ability to see clearly improves.

These life lessons from the tractor seat are just a few things that I have learned so far as a tractor driver.[1] Be looking for the life lessons that you can learn from your unique farm experience.

---

1 A version of, "Life Lessons from the Tractor Seat" appeared in January 2015 Successful Farming® Magazine. ©2015 Meredith Corporation. All rights reserved.

REFLECTIONS

COMMITMENTS

Makaley's "Bummer Lambs"

3

CONTINGENCY PLANS, WHO NEEDS 'EM?

---

*Everyone has a plan until they get
punched in the mouth.*

— MIKE TYSON

L ife on the farm is full of uncertainty. The only thing you can count on is that things will change and that you will have to adapt. Of all of the changes you might consider, it is important to know what you can control or influence and what you cannot. You can't control the weather or the price of commodities, but there are many things within your operation you can meticulously plan for. Jay Wolf, Past President of the Nebraska Cattlemen Association and owner of Wagonhammer Cattle shares about contingency planning, "It is too easy to procrastinate. Poorly executed business succession can do more long-term harm, financial and/or emotional, than a drought or market downturn."

Ownership and management contingency plans should not be thought of as optional. The only way for a family to own a farm in perpetuity is to begin with strong contingency plans.

SUCCESSION SUPERHEROES: WHAT SUPERHERO DO YOU RELATE TO?

After working with farmers and ranchers all over the United States, I have determined that there are four major 'superhero archetypes' that characterize how the majority of farmers feel about continuity.

Understanding these tendencies will help you to know how to deal with the uncertainty that surrounds you regarding ownership and management continuity. These superhero archetypes can be found in males and females alike, but I will characterize three as male and one as a female. Let me introduce you to our "Farm Succession Superheroes."

CAPTAIN IMMORTAL

He has hair that never grays, energy that never wanes and willpower seemingly stronger than life itself. The pursuit of success is both a passion and a seductress. While he is an intelligent man who at his core knows he will sometime vacate this mortal coil, he has convinced himself that day is years away, so investing time in planning or training the next generation is for now, an irrelevant task. Of course on this count, Captain Immortal lives only in the now.

DR. SHHHH

This superhero has a plan for the farm, but he values the power and freedom of privacy more than life itself. Dr. Shhhh enjoys the seclusion he finds in developing his proprietary business solutions. He does the same thing with his hopes and dreams for the future of his family and the farm. He knows that he is not completely immortal, but he doesn't want anyone else to realize it. In his mind he creates plans to continue the work he has silently pursued, but refuses to share those ideas with his wife and children. He feels that this affords him a great deal of freedom. He can modify his plans as circumstances play out and never upset anyone with a midstream shift. After all, why should he have to relinquish control and information before it is absolutely necessary?

OBLIVIOUS MAN

He is so consumed with doing his work that he doesn't even consider what will happen beyond his leadership of the farm, let alone consider the consequences. He goes about his superhero tasks, providing the necessities and luxuries of life for his family one day at a time. He has acquired a substantial reputation by virtue of the highly conscious manner in which he has built his operation over the years. On the other hand, he has no clue that he's laying the foundation for confusion, chaos and conflict for his family and employees by not making plans for the future of his farm.

MS. REALITY

This superhero has always been good at taking care of her business. While she enjoys the daily thrill of her work, she is highly aware that someday she will not be able to leap tall fences in a single bound or stop an oncoming bull with her bare hands. Ms. Reality has a strong drive to succeed personally, but she has an equally keen awareness of the responsibility that she must make long-term plans for her family and her farm. She is just as driven to create and execute her contingency plan as she is to succeed in the short-term because she sees planning as a critical and inevitable to longer-term success.

One uncertainty that every farmer faces is their ultimate death and its timing. It is almost comical to hear a "Captain Immortal-type" farmer say, "if I die or if I retire." It is important to remind farmers and ranchers that there is no "if" about either of those statements, only a when. While most people have some ideal in mind as to how they will live out their life, health issues, accidents and life in general can change those plans.

Two types of contingency plans need to receive special attention when it comes to perpetuating a generational farm. With each of these contingencies there are some critical questions to consider. Here are a few to help you get started.

Contingency Plans for Ownership Transition:

- How will ownership of assets flow when one of the current owners passes away?

- How has this expectation been communicated to the family and other important parties?

- What are the tax implications of this transition?

- How will your heirs feel about how you structured your plan for future ownership of the farm?

- How much debt will your heirs inherit and do you want to cover all or some of that with the purchase of life insurance?

Contingency Plans for Management Transition:

- If the top manager didn't show up on Monday and decisions on the farm needed to be made, who would make those choices?

- How big is the knowing/doing gap between the top leader and the next in charge regarding buying and selling cattle and the financial aspects of the cattle operation?

- What can you do now to minimize the risk inherent with much of the farmer's working knowledge being in the mind of the owner?

While creating these contingency plans for ownership and management seem straight forward, they are often difficult to complete for many farm owners. It all comes back to these superhero archetypes. So what do we do to "save our farming superheroes?"

CAPTAIN IMMORTAL

The key to rescuing Captain Immortal is to keep him from focusing on himself and get him to start focusing on immortalizing his legacy. Randy Johnson, an insurance professional of Ash Johnson in Ashland, NE shares, "Helping a farmer that sees themselves as immortal of the opportunity to make his legacy 'bulletproof' is a good first step to getting him to create a contingency plan."

One way to begin this process is to ask questions like, "What needs to happen over the next 20 years to be able to continue to call the farm a success?" Questions like these take the focus off of the person's mortality and move it towards the opportunity of creating an immortal legacy for the farm. While Captain Immortal-type farm owners may never acknowledge their own mortality, spending effort and energy on enabling him to celebrate and perpetuate his legacy will advance the planning necessary to protect his family and his business.

What needs to happen over the next 20 years to be able to continue to call the farm a success?

DR. SHHH

This superhero's biggest fear is that his long-term plans will not be accepted and embraced by all parties. Dr. Shhh is concerned about keeping the peace and not creating attitudes of entitlement in the next generation. He needs to understand that if he is no longer around to explain his hopes and motives, his desired outcome may never be achieved.

One question you might consider asking is, "What is the most important non-financial objective you hope to accomplish with your estate plan?" Randy Johnson explains that in his years working with farmers that, "Great questions take the focus off of the money and move it to the family and family dynamics, in other words... *why* does heartfelt planning matter?" As they vocalize those things, Dr. Shhh might become more comfortable sharing his wishes and dreams for the family and the farm. When he realizes that open communication is the best way to avoid negative consequences for the family and the farm, he will likely become less guarded.

~~~~~~

What is the most important non-financial objective you hope to accomplish with your estate plan?

~~~~~~

OBLIVIOUS MAN

The saving grace for Oblivious Man is his love for the farm and his family. He doesn't actively avoid planning; he just assigns a higher value to "getting the work done." Once he takes the time to begin working "on his farm business" rather than always working "in his farm business," the likelihood of accomplishing significant long-term planning and documenting his contingency plans for management and ownership increases dramatically.

~~~~~~

Begin working 'on his farm business' rather than always working 'in his farm business.'

~~~~~~

AVOIDING OUR OWN KRYPTONITE

Which superhero do you most relate to? What is your kryptonite? All of us have conflicts between what we need and want for ourselves and for our families. We constantly battle with what's expedient and prudent, between the easier path and the harder one, between our desire to live on and on and the reality that we are mortal. The question is: Do we deny these conflicts or take them head-on?[2] What contingency plans and long-term decisions should you be making for the benefit of your family farm?

---

2 A version of, "Contingency Plans, Who Needs 'Em" first appeared in Angus Journal in November 2014.

REFLECTIONS

COMMITMENTS

Nativity Scene Gone Wrong – 2008

4

'I'M NOT A SHEEP!'—THE CHALLENGES OF FITTING IN

*Management is doing things right,
leadership is doing the right things.*

—PETER DRUCKER

It's Christmas Eve at grandma's house the extended family has gathered and is preparing to re-enact the Nativity. Little girls fight over who will be the gentle Mary, and in-laws draw straws for the role of the donkey. My 2-year-old son walks into the room with a white apron tied on like a cape over his shoulders and sporting a white ruffled lace bonnet. He has, obviously, been dressed by one of his young aunts to be a makeshift sheep. The only problem was that he isn't buying the idea.

I remark that he makes a very nice looking sheep, he quickly turns to me with a fierce scowl, and in his little gruff voice proclaims, "I am not a sheep, I'm a superhero!"

At that moment I realize that while the family has an idea of how my son should fit into the story, he is not interested. He went along with it long enough to get a costume, but that was it. How many times does this happen in a family business?

"I am not a sheep, I'm a superhero!"

One example of this challenge took place with an impressive student mine at the University of Nebraska. After the first day of class Betsy came up to me and confessed that she had no intention of returning to the family business. Her only reason for taking a course in Family Business was because her father told her she needed to. At that point she was looking to me to tell her that she shouldn't take the class, but I didn't let her off that easy.

The business that her family owns is called Speedway Motors and it is known throughout the United States as "America's Oldest Speed Shop." She explained to me that she didn't have a natural interest in dirt track racing and didn't see herself fitting in the male dominated sport. I listened, but having a passion for preserving family businesses I think everyone should take my class. And because I truly believe in the power of family run businesses on so many levels, Betsy couldn't have sought out a worse ally if she wanted to drop my class.

Fast forward just six months and Betsy discovered that her passion for social media and marketing is the avenue by which she could carve out a niche in the industry and add real value to Speedway Motors. In just a couple of years she would build a thriving online business and social media platform that are valuable in a way that no one, even herself, could have foreseen.

At times, parents in pride and anticipation tell their kids, "Someday you will own this business." And I just picture my disgruntled son saying, "I am not a sheep, I am a superhero."

Do business owners ever consider the fact that their dream might not be their child's? In Betsy's case she had to discover that her talents and passion could be applied to the family business. Do parents listen to their children enough to know what they really should be encouraging them to pursue?

A family can have the most profitable hot dog factory in the state or the most successful farm in the country, but does the next generation have enough of a passion for hot dogs or farming to carry the torch? Multi-generational success in business happens when multiple generations are passionate about the same business. Cash flow and profitability aside, a genuine interest and love for the farm is essential for successful continuity.

Multi-generational success in business happens when multiple generations are passionate about the same business.

How do you develop in and encourage your children to discover their passion? No one wants to watch someone they love grind away at a job they despise simply out of a sense of duty. Nor is that the best scenario for farm productivity or happy family relations. Luckily, in the world we live in there is no limit to the opportunities for creating job niches that are customized to maximize talent and utilize training where there is desire and a willingness to work hard.

Here are five tips followed by a deeper exploration of each:

- Always speak positively about the farm
- Bring children along as much as

possible when they are young

- Have other trusted employees work with your children as they are developing

- Expose children to different aspects of the farming operation and see how they respond

- Talk about what owning a farm allows you to do for the community and the family

Speaking positively about the farm is one of the easiest things a parent can do to create goodwill in the mind of a child. Frequent complaining about the farm and how tough things are will surely discourage potential future owners from wanting to carry on the family operation. The old saying, "If you don't have anything nice to say, don't say anything at all," has real application if your intent is to attract your child or children to someday join the family farm.

Including children at an early age is usually a very positive experience for them and will create memories that link them to the farm. Angie Muhleisen, President of Union Bank and Trust in Lincoln, NE agrees saying, "I grew up hearing my father talk about banking around the family dinner table. Even though I didn't realize it at the time, these conversations taught me a lot about banking and were the catalyst for my life-long interest in the profession." Being proud of the family business and allowing children to be around as much as possible builds ties to the operation that someday might be strong enough to make them want to come back and join or even lead it.

As children have their first experiences in the family business, allowing them to live what goes on out there, while not always under the watchful eye of mom or dad is important. Family Business thought leader and Professor at Brigham Young University, Gibb Dyer explains, "I have found that finding a nonfamily mentor for family members to be extremely valuable in helping them develop their talents and get the feedback they need to grow and improve." Choosing a trusted employee to mentor and befriend them may be the difference in pushing children away from the farm or encouraging them to gravitate back towards it.

Exposing the next generation to many aspects of the operation is important for a couple of reasons. First, it gives children an opportunity to learn what they like most about the farm and what they enjoy least. It also gives the senior generation a chance to see the next generation's natural talent or inclinations to certain areas of the operation. Finding the right fit is key to retaining and inspiring the next generation to stay with the farm and grow in their leadership abilities.

Lastly, it is important to not only talk about the farm itself, but to talk about the benefits and opportunities that farm ownership provides for you individually and for the family. Speak of the importance of the farm in the community and share the charitable and civic opportunities that you have had because you are a farmer. Express your gratitude about the benefits of owning a farm, especially those that seem unrelated, and are not always clearly visible to the next generation.

Remember, when you are growing your farming operation and introducing the next generation to it, don't assume that just because you've got them in the apron and bonnet that they will want to be a sheep. The last thing you want is for a child to return to the farm and then have them tell you, "I am not a sheep, I am a superhero." Encourage, train, and mentor them if that is their inclination, but let it be their passion.[3] Then the family farm will have a good chance to survive and even thrive for multiple generations.

---

3 A version of, "I'm Not a Sheep" originally appeared in Nebraska Bankers Magazine in January 2011.

REFLECTIONS

_____

_____

_____

_____

_____

_____

_____

_____

COMMITMENTS

_____

_____

_____

_____

2015 Washington State FFA Convention

5

FFA–'FOREVER FARMHANDS OF AMERICA'

*There is an expiry date on blaming your parents
for steering you in the wrong direction;
the moment you are old enough to take the
wheel, responsibility lies with you.*

–J.K. ROWLING

As a "farm kid from San Diego" I was lucky to be in 4-H and to raise pigs for the Del Mar Fair. I learned the value of caring for an animal, and discipline with routine feedings and cleanings. I also learned about the power of good marketing--my red ribbon pig ended up making higher then market value money, much to my sister's chagrin, when I came up with an advertising campaign based around my pig's similar appearance to the popular beer commercial dog, Spud Mackenzie. While I realize now that growing up on 2.5 acres and having a couple of pigs in 4-H doesn't necessarily make me a true farmer, it did teach me some important lessons.

When high school arrived, I missed out on the FFA experience because of distractions like basketball and a driver's license. Though I wasn't involved in the Future Farmers of America in high school, I appreciated the lessons that were taught to the young men and women that were. I saw many of my friends develop skills in public speaking, finance and leadership that would have benefitted me greatly.

Now, as a father of five small children I hope to teach the values and lessons available in 4-H and FFA. In my career as a strategy consultant to family farms and ranches across the country I am alarmed by what I am seeing. FFA stands for "Future Farmers of America", yet all too often I am seeing young people return to their farm with no formal growth plan. The tragic result is that many fall back into the role of hired grunt. I worry about the talented youth who have sought education and experience only to be positioned as the "Forever Farmhands of America."

To illustrate, years ago I was approached by a man that had seen my writings or heard me speak and he asked if I could help his family organize a contingency plan for their family feedlot. I told him I would be happy to work with the family and their professionals to put something together. He then warned me that his dad was "a little controlling" and it may be a challenge. At that point I thought to myself, "I like challenges" and I told him I would meet with them. So the agreed upon day came and I drove out to the feedlot and met the man I visited with on the phone. He had two brothers that also worked with him and their father on the feedlot.

*...with no formal growth plan the tragic result is
that many fall back into the role of hired grunt...*

Things started off great as I met with the brothers and listened to what they wanted to see happen. Then it got interesting. The sons introduced me to their father. This man was in his early 80s, walked the feed bunks every day to pick up any feed that fell from the troughs as the cattle fed and getting him to smile was like pushing a rope. Early on I could tell that he didn't trust me and that he wasn't going to take advice from anyone.

My conversation with him began by asking him how he got started in the business and I quickly learned why he was so controlling. He shared with me how in the early years he would go into town each night and sneak behind the restaurant where he would gather up the chicken necks that had been thrown out so that he would have something to take home to feed his boys. He told me of the risk and the hardship in building the feedlot over the many years. He then shared with me that, "This feedlot will not fail under my watch." I then learned that, "the boys" as he referred to them had never been allowed to buy or sell cattle. I couldn't believe it! "The boys" were all in their 50s and they didn't know the nuances of the most important part of the business. Well, needless to say my engagement with this family was not a successful one, but I did learn some new words out there behind that old feedlot building, so I guess I could thank the man for that.

One thing I did take away from that experience was a resolve to teach the next generation what they should ask before returning to the family operation. I committed to helping educate future farmers in such a way that they could know if there really was a true leadership and ownership opportunity for them on their farm.

In order to avoid this terrible situation on your farm, families must do four things for their young, ambitious talent that wants to return.

- Develop a formal job description for the youth that come back. Give them real responsibility and the opportunity to make meaningful decisions. Create an expectation that their performance will be measured and that they will receive regular feedback.

- Instill in the younger generation an attitude of ownership. Involve them as early as possible in the financial realities of the farm. Allow them to begin to share risk in purchases of livestock, equipment and even farm ground as soon as possible.

- Talk about compensation openly and directly. Have a candid discussion about what you will pay them. Talk about all aspects of the benefits that are available to them. If housing, fuel, insurance, food and other perks are a part of the compensation, talk about those things directly as a part of the whole package. Let them know that if you plan to pay them below market wages that you will understand if they choose to pursue a different career.

- Have an open dialogue about the future. It is crucial to talk about issues regarding shared ownership, inheritance expectations, the timing of when and if they can buy into the farm, etc.

America needs FFA to truly and completely mean "Future Farmers of America", not "Forever Farmhands of America." Do the hard work now to make sure your family is positioning the next generation to understand what it takes to be a successful farmer. Ask the hard questions and if you need help, there's an app for that. It's called

Inspired Questions—For Farmers. *(Available for iOS on the App Store and for Android on Google Play)*

REFLECTIONS

_____

_____

_____

_____

_____

_____

_____

_____

_____

_____

_____

COMMITMENTS

_____

_____

_____

_____

"Libby's John Deere 790"

6

---

5 DANGERS FARMERS SHOULD AVOID DURING GOOD TIMES

Debt is normal. Be weird.

—DAVE RAMSEY

For the past several years farming, for most, has been a very profitable venture. If your operation includes members who have returned to the farm in the last five years, it may be easy for them to assume this kind of prosperity is the norm. It is during times like these you should consider some of the risks that accompany prosperous times. When commodity prices are good, asset values are sky high and the weather cooperates, it is easy to get sloppy. Don't be the one who is lulled into forgetting just how hard things can get. While the future continues to look bright, you might consider these five dangers that can quickly turn parasitic in lean times.

LAND RUSH!—BUYING EXPENSIVE FARM GROUND

When the farm is profitable most farmers aren't thinking about paying themselves a higher wage, diversifying their investment portfolio or pursuing the luxuries of the day. Most farmers want more ground. In this environment of soaring land values, it is easy to say to one's self, "they aren't making more land and if we are going to survive in the future, we will need to get more of it."

While this statement may be true, the timing of when you purchase that land will greatly determine the opportunities for profitability and growth into the future. Paying too much for ground and assuming that values will continue to rise indefinitely may be a recipe for disaster. Pay close attention to the land profitability now, calculate for future market downturns or commodity price pullbacks.

IRON FEVER!—OVER-LEVERAGING THE FARM WITH NEW EQUIPMENT

Everyone loves a shiny new tractor on the farm and it may increase efficiency or allow you to farm more acres. New equipment can bring technology and other drivers of progress but take care to view equipment in the proper context.

Jeff Gerhart, President of Bank of Newman Grove in Nebraska and Past Chairman of the Independent Community Bankers of America says, "Guarding against emotion buying is key, but it's also in our DNA."

Jeff classifies this desire to buy new equipment as "iron fever" and it seems to spread quickly among friends and neighbors. Farm equipment should be seen as a way to farm more efficiently and more profitably long-term. Be wary of wanting a tractor or combine in much the same way as you should avoid buying a car just to "keep up with the Joneses."

It is best to make equipment purchases as a part of an ongoing plan. Obviously when needs arise for newer equipment, you will have to make those decisions, but trading up just to have new equipment could lead to strained finances down the road.

MONEY, MONEY, MONEY!–GROWING PAYROLL

If you were a child during the 1980's you probably were not encouraged by your parents to get into farming. High interest rates and poor farm profitability led most parents to suggest their children find an alternate career choice. The exact opposite is true today. Farming has been a successful venture for many families, interest rates are historically low, commodity prices have remained solid and many young people are beginning to look at agriculture as a great business opportunity. Many are also recognizing after working in a corporate job that life on the farm is simply a wonderful way to raise a family.

During good times there is a tendency to invite family members back to the farm, because the farm can afford it. Also, while this doesn't happen much, farmers may begin to actually pay themselves substantially more. We should teach our next generation that the farm didn't grow and become prosperous by taking most of the cash out of the business.

Tim Cobb, of Hatley/Cobb Farm Management in Spokane, WA shares, "the overall compensation package will be hard to retract when times get tough so be conservative and speak openly about just what the compensation arrangement include." Tim suggests looking at the compensation from an apples-to-apples comparison. Some farm-employees compensation includes housing, fuel, a vehicle, health insurance and other perks. The danger is only looking at the wage and then comparing it to non-farm jobs. Tim sees the best farm managers making those important compensation decisions based on merit and on solid financial models for the farm.

RATE BLINDNESS!–INTEREST RATE RISK

One of the toughest things to manage is the unknown cost of variable expenses. Potentially the most challenging changes are the cost of financing equipment, ongoing operations and land. It is especially difficult to have a good sense for just how much is at risk when interest rates have been at record lows for such an extended period of time.

Gerhart cautions, "Interest rates have been too low for too long. This gives everyone a false sense of security and that's not good." The biggest danger is to assume that financing will continue to be available in this range forever. As you consider the costs of operating profitable farm, ask yourself what would it do to the farm if rates rose by a percentage point or more? Gerhart believes that "It is important to 'stress test' the business model to have clarity for the types of changes and challenges that the farm will face in the future." Jeff shares the recent example of $7.00 per bushel corn in 2013. Today, just one year later, it is $4.00 per bushel. "How does your farm profitability look with price declines like these?"

NECESSARY WANTS!–INCREASING THE FLEET OF MOTORIZED FUN

Tim Cobb also warns against the temptation to "increase the size of the fleet of motorized fun." The farm affords many to purchase motorcycles, John Deere Gators and even boats or RVs. While you might be able to convince the IRS that these are necessary business expenses, your financial statements will not be so kind to you when commodity prices fall, interest rates rise or other unforeseen events occur that squeeze profit margins.

It is best to focus your purchasing on income producing assets, even when times are good. This isn't to say that you shouldn't buy toys, but you will need to use judgment and wisdom, especially when it feels like the farm can easily afford the toys.

Today's farmers are living through some of the most prosperous times in history. In these times it is vital to remember the struggles and business cycles of the past, anticipating proof in the adage that 'history repeats itself'.[4] While it is important to live in the present and plan for the future, we should take a lesson and never be blindsided by our own successes.

Focus on what risks you can control, be aware of the risks that can effect your farm that you cannot control and plan to allow your operation to maintain the kind of liquidity and flexibility to weather whatever storms may be on the horizon.

---

4 "5 Things Farmers Should Avoid During Good Times" is an article from August 2015 Successful Farming® Magazine. ©2015 Meredith Corporation. All rights reserved.

REFLECTIONS

_____

_____

_____

_____

_____

_____

_____

_____

_____

_____

COMMITMENTS

_____

_____

_____

_____

2015 Branding @ Van Newkirk's

7

ENTICED OR HERDED—FARM CONTINUITY PLANNING

BE MISERABLE. OR MOTIVATE YOURSELF.
WHATEVER HAS TO BE DONE, IT'S ALWAYS YOUR CHOICE.

—WAYNE DYER

Watching a skilled cowboy move cattle from one pasture to another, it becomes clear that there are certain things that motivate the cattle to go where he wants them to go. Sometimes the cowhands are a tornado of constant motion and noise employing every tactic in their arsenal to force a stubborn herd in the right direction. Other times they trail along behind the cattle at a lazy lope, whistling a tune and enjoying the sunshine and wild flowers.

During such observations, you might see some correlations between farm families and their ability to get continuity plans in place for their farms. While some families struggle to make meaningful progress, others move through their plan easily, steadily progressing towards the goals that will help their families to perpetuate their generational operations.

In comparing moving cattle to watching farm families put continuity plans in place, I find that there are three major correlations.

CATTLE FOLLOW EACH OTHER AND MOVE IN HERDS

Just as cattle many times follow the lead of others, so do farmers who watch respected peers take steps in moving forward in planning for the continuity of their farm. Boyd Clyde, a cattlemen from Connell, WA shares, "It is important that when you are moving cattle to know when to apply pressure to get them moving and when to release that pressure and allow them to move on their own."

Similarly, it may take family members or professional advisers to "apply some pressure" or encouragement regarding continuity planning and then know when to back off to allow the controlling owner to make choices and to move forward on their own. Just as when a cowboy applies too much pressure, a controlling owner can get frustrated and stop the process all together.

CATTLE ARE MOTIVATED BY FOOD, WATER AND SHELTER

Some cowboys that work cattle motivate them by moving them towards a feed source. If the cow knows there is something there for them, generally they are more willing to cooperate. Farmers, in much the same way, will move towards making their plans when there is something that will satisfy a desire, like tax minimization or some other tangible benefit.

COWS ARE MOTIVATED BY THEIR CALVES

If following the herd or food doesn't work, cowboys sometimes will use the calf as motivation to get a stubborn cow to go where they want it to go. A good mother cow will always follow her calf. Randy Johnson, a life insurance expert from Ashland, NE shares, "The desire to leave the people they care most about in a good situation creates action." If the farmer senses that the son or daughter is in danger of failing or being caused undue stress due to the lack of planning, that may be just what is needed to get the process going.

What will motivate you or your parents to take action in establishing a continuity plan for your farm or ranch? Will it be the influence of a friend?[5] Will it be the opportunity to minimize taxes or accomplish some other personal goal, or will it be the love for your children that will cause you to get a plan in place?

It doesn't matter which of these things motivates you to take action, it's that you do something towards establishing a continuity plan for the ownership and management of the farm. Don't be a stubborn cow, get going now!

---

5 A version of "Enticed or Herded" originally appeared in Nebraska Farmer Magazine in July 2014.

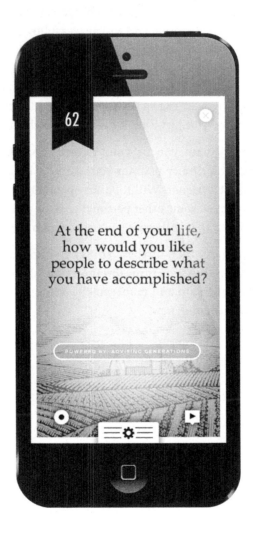

At the end of your life, how would you like people to describe what you have accomplished?

REFLECTIONS

_____

_____

_____

_____

_____

_____

_____

_____

_____

_____

COMMITMENTS

_____

_____

_____

_____

HALFTIME ENTERTAINMENT

Don't give up at half time.
Concentrate on winning the second half.

—PAUL BRYANT

Jhett's Broken Leg and Baby On The Way

8

10 THINGS A FARMER SHOULD NEVER SAY TO HIS PREGNANT WIFE[6]

Freedom of speech does not protect you from the consequences of saying something stupid.

—JIM C. HINES

Throughout history men have been known to say some foolish things, some were subsequently beheaded for it. If you are interested in avoiding beheading, wake up and pay attention! Here are 10 things a man should NEVER say to their pregnant wife.

---

6   A version of "10 Things a Farmers Should Never Say to His Pregnant Wife" originally appeared on FamilyShare.com in July 2014.

1 **Man I slept good last night!**

Women do not want to hear this. Pregnancy is an uncomfortable time for a woman. Sleep is scarce and almost always interrupted by glamorous things like acid reflux and frequent trips to the bathroom.

2 **I know how you feel.**

No you don't! This statement of attempted empathy doesn't work, so don't even go there.

3 **Don't you think one bowl of ice cream is enough?**

Mothers-to-be often enjoy comfort foods and ice cream is one of them. Cut them some slack and don't make the mistake of monitoring portions or critiquing requests for strange food combinations. If she asks for pickles and peanut butter at 1 a.m., give the woman what she wants!

4 **I think you might have stretched out my favorite pair of shorts.**

While this may be true, you should never say it. Pregnant women will do just about anything to be comfortable, including stealing your favorite gym shorts.

5 **Your toes make me hungry for sausage!**

Most women experience uncomfortable swelling in their legs and feet during pregnancy. If your wife struggles with this, keep your comments to yourself, unless you enjoy your evenings alone sleeping on the couch.

6 **Whoa, did one of the kids write on your leg with blue marker?**

Varicose veins are often one of the burdens some women have to endure during pregnancy. No comment about varicose veins is welcome, so avoid that conversation all together.

7 Why are you crying...again?

When women are pregnant their hormones can fluctuate. Don't assume they need a "reason" to cry. If you want to help, just offer a shoulder to cry on.

8 I think it would be fun if our kids were a year apart.

This comment may quickly transform the woman you love into a raging monster. Appreciate the pain and sacrifice she is going through both physically and mentally and don't assume she wants to repeat the experience anytime soon.

9 Epidurals are getting so expensive. I think WE should go natural.

Yes, epidurals cost money, but don't ever include a "we" when talking to your wife about natural childbirth. There is no "we," it's just her.

10 It feels like you've been pregnant forever.

This could get you a bloody nose. No one feels like the pregnancy is longer than the woman. This is a no-win comment that also should be avoided at all costs.

Think before you speak, and just as every parent tells his child, "If you don't have something nice to say, don't say anything at all."

Me, Grandma Gibbons and Dr. Seuss

9

THE QUIET KILLER OF THE GENERATIONAL FARM

By failing to prepare, you are preparing to fail.

—BENJAMIN FRANKLIN

T he farm is worth more than ever and commodity prices look good right now. Why in the world would I need to consider long-term care insurance?" Does this conversation opener sound familiar? If it does, you aren't alone. For Jim Wagner, a long-term care expert from Lincoln, NE, reports that this is pretty typical. Jim shares, "While many farmers and ranchers are focused on ownership and management transitions, the possibility of a long-term care event is not usually on the radar for things to worry about. Most believe it will never happen to them, but statistics show that 60-70% of people will need care at some time."

As a farmer or rancher, there are a few key elements to generational succession. First, you need to have a next generation that is both capable and interested. Second, you need to have a farm that provides plenty of cash flow to fulfil the needs of the retiring generation and the next generation that is returning to run the operation. Third, you need to communicate the intentions and expectations to all parties so that plans are understood and can be carried out.

~~~~~~

60—70% of people will need some sort of long-term care

~~~~~~

It is important to consider these three keys, but a farm or ranch can easily be derailed in the cash flow portion of the plan if a need for long-term care arises. Wagner explains, "There are a few essential elements to these types of policies that farmers and ranchers should understand before they purchase."

"WHAT TYPE OF COVERAGE AM I INTERESTED IN?"

Depending on the policy that you purchase you may be able to buy coverage that allows you to receive in-home care, not just typical nursing home care. This flexibility is often desired by independent minded people like farmers and ranchers if it is an option. There are many arguments behind the idea that quality of life is preferable lived out in ones own home as opposed to a forced move into a care facility.

"HOW MUCH COVERAGE SHOULD I PURCHASE?"

The answer to this question depends on a few factors. What type of a facility are you comfortable living in? Do you want a private room or are you willing to share a room? What is a proper amount of coverage that you can afford, while not neglecting the other planning needs of the farm? According to the 2014 Genworth Cost of Care Study, national median daily rate for a nursing home facility is $240 per day. That calclulates to $87,600 a year, not an insignificant sum. With these types of costs, the farm or ranch must decide how much it can afford to cover out of cash flow and how much of the cost it would make sense to insure.

National Median nursing home facility care costs = $87,600 annually

"WHAT HAS TO HAPPEN FOR ME TO BEGIN RECEIVING BENEFITS FROM THE POLICY?"

According to Wagner there are a six activities of daily living that are typically used as criteria that will trigger the payment of benefits. Most policies specify that if you cannot perform a certain number of the activities of daily living that benefits will begin. Activities of daily living consist of getting dressed without assistance, being able to eat and also use the restroom independently. Having the ability to bathe and transfer in and out of a chair or wheelchair unaided would also be considered. Finally, the ability to manage incontinence without assistance is deemed a necessary activity of daily living.

So, do farmers really need long-term care insurance? The answer is maybe. Depending on your family situation, your family's ability to provide care and your cash flow situation, it may be something to consider.[7] Choosing to ignore the issue is not planning for it. Take a careful look at your circumstances, talk to your family and move forward with deciding how to cover the risk of long-term care jeopardizing the continuity of your family farm.

---

7   A version of "The Quiet Killer of the Family Farm" is an article from September 2014 Successful Farming® Magazine. ©2014 Meredith Corporation. All rights reserved.

REFLECTIONS

_____

_____

_____

_____

_____

_____

_____

_____

_____

_____

COMMITMENTS

_____

_____

_____

_____

Thett & Libby - Learning to Share

10

THE UNINTENDED CONSEQUENCES OF SHARED OWNERSHIP

---

*As a leader your every action has a consequence,
make sure it is an intended one.*

−KATHERINE BRYANT

Everyone loves the family farm, the independence, the flexibility, working the land, love, love, love it . . . until you have to share ownership and make operating decisions with a non-operating sibling. Choosing to come back and work the farm represents an opportunity for independence and an avenue to avoid the corporate bureaucracy that your non-farming friends have to deal with in their jobs. Then it happens, mom or dad passes away and you learn their estate plan calls for you to share ownership with your sister who has an office job in Chicago.

~~~~~~

Shared ownership is the toughest thing that you
can ask a human being to do

~~~~~~

While, from your parents perspective, this seems like the logical and fair way to transition ownership, it introduces a new complexity into your life. Randy Johnson, an insurance specialist from Ashland, NE explains, "Shared ownership is the toughest thing that you can ask a human being to do, especially with a farming operation." If you think back to when you were a kid, imagine having to share ownership in a car with your not-so caring brother. You may have different ideas about mechanical maintenance. You may not share the same standards of cleanliness and overall upkeep. One of you may seem to always leave the gas tank mostly empty. All of these differences can lead to conflict and may even be detrimental to the long-term value of the car.

Sharing ownership in a farm is even more complex. It may entail decisions about equipment purchases, land use, marketing decisions and financing needs. These are all critical for the long-term health of the farm and reaching consensus on each of these items is essential. While it is likely that all siblings love the farm, it is not likely that all share the same perspective on these issues.

If shared ownership is the path for your family, it will be important for each party to know their rights, responsibilities and accept their roles. It is also important for each family to have a way for members of the family to sell their interest in the farm in a way that gives the farm an opportunity to maintain its family ownership, while providing a fair price for the family member that wants out.

Johnson's experience working with farmers teaches him that, "Transparency and a communicated plan for how families can unwind these sibling ownership structures is crucial to preserving relationships and perpetuating the farming operation across generations." Shared ownership can be emotionally challenging and can make the best communicators feel a little uneasy. The last thing you want is to have family members feel as if they are being held hostage by the family farm.

Here are three ways to minimize risk with shared ownership relationships.

- Create a clear understanding of the rights and obligations of ownership in the farm for operators and non-operators.

- Develop a consistent and structured pattern of communication around central issues relating to the long-term success of the operation. (Example: Semi-annual meetings to update non-operating family members)

- Avoid shared ownership obligations when family members vary significantly in the areas of risk taking and personality differences.

While it seems to be the goal of every parent to treat their children fairly and with love, shared ownership in the farming operation isn't always the best way to communicate that feeling. Take time to understand the true challenges with forcing your children into a shared ownership situation and then put together a plan and communicate your intentions for the farm and for the family.[8] Shared ownership may work well for many, but make sure that you are going into it with your eyes wide open.

---

8 A version of "Unintended Consequences of Shared Ownership" is an article from December 2013 Successful Farming® Magazine. ©2013 Meredith Corporation. All rights reserved.

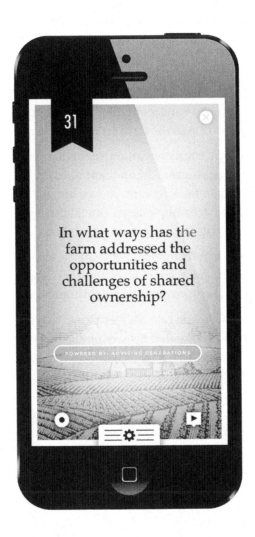

REFLECTIONS

_____

_____

_____

_____

_____

_____

_____

_____

_____

_____

COMMITMENTS

_____

_____

_____

_____

Neighbor Family @ Van Newkirk's Bull Sale

11

GENERATIONAL BUSINESS 360

*We do not see things as they are,
we see things as we are.*

— ANAIS NIN

In order to preserve America's most precious asset, family farms and businesses, advisors must know where gaps in perceptions exist between spouses and between generations. When beginning to work with new customers, I evaluate seven themes in a process I have named Generational Business 360™.

BUSINESS AND ESTATE PLANNING

There are a few aspects of transferring a farm that make it crucial to have a solid estate plan in place. In addition to having a plan that incorporates strategies to minimize taxes and facilitate an orderly transfer of assets, a good estate plan should also account for the management and ownership needs that may exist within the farm.

The best plans are developed when a team of trusted professionals including a CPA, an attorney, an insurance professional, a wealth manager and a banker work together with a family to develop a plan. This strategy ensures a plan that not only accomplishes the farm needs but also provides for the needs of the family.

Tax laws and family needs are always changing, so a good estate plan should also provide a level of flexibility that allows the plan to adapt over time. Individuals should reanalyze their estate plans periodically and make necessary adjustments as circumstances change. Performing a routine review of an estate plan may also help identify additional planning opportunities where business interests may be transferred in the most economical manner.

COMMUNICATION

Communication of intentions and dreams of both the senior generation and the next generation is critical, but that can sometimes be difficult. However, the ability to work through challenges while speaking respectfully is crucial to the success of any family farm. Families that set aside time to discuss the business and the goals for the family will increase their likelihood of success.

Focusing on working through these challenges is the most important first step you can take in helping to preserve your family farm.

LEADERSHIP DEVELOPMENT

Grooming family members in the next generation to run the farm takes both initiative and patience. An intentional skill development plan that encompasses both education and experience will give young family members the necessary abilities and confidence to allow the senior generation to delegate meaningful responsibility when the time is right. Creating expectations and accountability will aid them in their growth.

TRUST

There are many types of trust that need to be in place for a generational transfer to be successful. Members of the senior generation must trust the decision-making ability of the next generation in both personal and business life. They must also trust that the younger family members have similar goals for the future of the farm.

Equally important is the next generation's level of trust in the senior generation regarding intentions for the future. If either side doesn't trust the other, the process of transitioning the business will most likely break down.

PERSONAL RESILIENCE

Just as personal resilience is one of the elements that make a farm successful to begin with, it is also essential for the continued success of a business. Effective owners know how to learn from their mistakes, embrace change, and do not give up when things are difficult. If the next generation doesn't have a great deal of personal resilience, things might not go as expected.

It's best to find out early if someone intended to take over the farm isn't wired to be an owner. If this is the case, more focus must be placed on developing a support network to help the future owner successfully manage the operation.

RETIREMENT AND INVESTMENT PLANNING

Most successful farmers have one common challenge—they are usually asset rich but relatively cash poor. When considering the prospect of transitioning out of the operation, the senior generation's retirement cash flow sources and needs should be carefully planned for. It should be determined what the desire for cash flow is, and that expectation should be measured against the ability of the operation to create it. Families who want farm continuity through the generations would be wise to do everything they can to create alternative sources of retirement cash flow.

Does the farm create enough cash flow to support all the working families and comfortable retirees?

KEY NON-FAMILY EMPLOYEES

In farm succession, key nonfamily employees are sometimes the most important piece of the puzzle. Taking the opportunity to share the family's visions and dreams for the future with key employees can instill confidence and loyalty in a group that will ultimately help navigate the operation through the most difficult part of the transition. Sometimes communicating with key employees is enough, but other times financial incentives are used to entice them to help the family make the transition successfully.

Each family has unique issues in its generational transfer situations. But if you can identify the strengths, weaknesses, and gaps in perception with the seven themes of the Generational Business 360™ process, you will increase the likelihood for success.[9] Focusing on working through these challenges with all family members is key in the preservation of America's most precious asset, the family farm.

---

9   A version of "Generational Business 360™" first appeared in The Edge Magazine in May 2012.

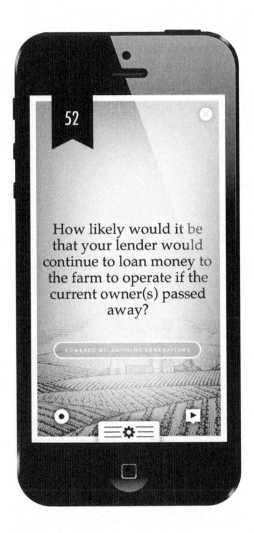

REFLECTIONS

COMMITMENTS

Makaley's Big Payday

12

THE COMPENSATION CONUNDRUM

*Therefore all things whatsoever ye would that men
should do unto you, do you even so to them.*

— MATTHEW 7:12

D ad, we need to have a talk about my salary. I think I should be
paid more for the work I do."

"Son, when I was your age I didn't take a paycheck for six
months to get this farm started, and then when it got going I paid
myself as little as possible to be able to buy land and equipment."

Sound familiar? If it does, you are not alone. On the family
farm there are stages that not only cause challenges but require
attention, effort and, perhaps most painful of all things, change.
Compensation is one of those areas that needs to be discussed

openly and should of necessity evolve over time.

STAGES OF THE FAMILY FARM

Most family farms start as an organization that may have one employee and a couple of unpaid helpers otherwise known as children and/or spouse. If the farm survives the first generation, more family members may return to the farm, requiring more structure and processes to be introduced. As the farm grows beyond the founder, job descriptions should be developed, some non-family talent may be hired and their compensation is determined based on the competitive landscape of the marketplace.

If the farm continues to grow and talented non-family employees that are key to the ongoing success of the business get recognized as valuable assets, compensation packages develop to incentivize them to be loyal and to continue to grow with the farm. This progression happens on the family farm just like in any other organization, except it is not always the same for family members that work in the operation.

Compensation needs to be discussed openly and should of necessity evolve over time.

The experience of the founder and the memory of when things were tight doesn't fade fast and so when the next generation comes back and expects to be paid a market wage for the job they perform, there is increased potential for a disconnect. At times it is perceived that the senior generation is being "unfair" or too tight with the purse strings while the next generation is accused of wanting too much, too fast. While both of these lines of reasoning may be true in some situations, they are not valid in all cases.

The senior generation expects the next generation to make sacrifices similar to theirs, reasoning such sacrifices are directly correlated to their subsequent success. The next generation feels the need to be treated fairly from a salary perspective because they are simply not positioned to "win" in the same way as their parents when the farm is successful. The next generation doesn't necessarily benefit financially when the farm's value grows.

Aaron Schardt, the Senior Vice President of the agriculture-focused, Heartland Bank Trust Department in Geneva, Nebraska shares, "Communication between the generations is crucial because ownership is sometimes slow to come, and so there is strain between the current compensation arrangements and the ultimate ownership strategy of the senior generation."

WHAT IS YOUR TRUE COMPENSATION PACKAGE?

To begin this conversation, both generations should have a clear understanding of what the true compensation package is. For example, in agriculture it is sometimes the case that housing, utilities, transportation and even the use of acreage is made available to the next generation without paying market, or sometimes any, rent at all. If this is the case, it should be considered part of the compensation package. If cars, trucks, fuel and other benefits are a part of the package, they should also be included in the discussion.

It is important that both generations recognize what the other considers part of the compensation package.

Example: Son complains to his friend that he is only paid a $2,000

per month wage for working on the family farm and he puts in
60-70 hours per week and is expected to not take vacations or time
away. In the same case the father may complain to his buddies that
his son doesn't appreciate the rich compensation package that his
son has. "We pay for his housing, electricity, water, his pickup and
fuel, his kids have horses that we feed and we still pay him $2,000
per month, and he still doesn't think it's enough."

Both generations must work to understand the needs and perspectives of the other, and discuss what will work for them and what they value. The next generation needs to take into consideration the lifestyle and benefits that they have and use fair comparisons when they look at the compensation of their peers.

The compensation conversation is always a tough one. The balance of being competitive with pay, while assuring that the farm is viable is a challenge. The reality of the senior generation's "true" compensation package should also be considered. Did they really just pay themselves a measly salary with no upside when the company performed well? If the next generation isn't participating in the upside of when the business is profitable, should their pay really be compared to what the senior generation's pay was when they started farming?

HOW MUCH IS TOO MUCH?

There are a couple of different scenarios that farm-owning families face with compensation. One is not paying family members enough for the role they fulfill; the other is paying them too much.

Family Wealth Advisor Paul Comstock from Houston, Texas cautions families to "pay a market wage for the job description that is outlined. It shouldn't matter if the role is filled by a family member or not, the role should be paid at market wage." Paul warns about the conflicts that arise from not compensating according to the specific role the family member fills.

~~~~~~~~~~~~~~~~~~~~~~~~~~~~~~~~~~~~

It shouldn't matter if the role is filled by a family member or not, the role should be paid at market wage.

~~~~~~~~~~~~~~~~~~~~~~~~~~~~~~~~~~~~

Here are three possible challenges that Mr. Comstock sees in working with business owning families regarding compensation.

- The next generation feels like they are getting something they don't deserve and this actually will hurt their confidence in the long-run.

- The non-family employees who are peers will come to resent the family member that is treated better while doing the same type of work.

- The farm begins to be treated less like a competitive business and more like a family piggy bank leading to the ultimate downfall of the operation.

These are challenges for each farm-owning family to confront. The fairest compensation package is the one that is discussed in "apples to apples" terms in a respectful and open manner. When the generations appreciate the contributions of each other and when both are focused on adding more value to the farm than their compensation package warrants is when success and harmony are found.[10] Avoid the compensation conundrum by facing these issues head on and putting a plan together that is fair, competitive and communicated.

---

10 A version of "The Compensation Conundrum" is an article from December 2013 *Successful Farming*® Magazine. ©2013 Meredith Corporation. All rights reserved.

From a cash flow perspective, how ready is the farm today to have another family come back to join the farm?

REFLECTIONS

_____

_____

_____

_____

_____

_____

_____

_____

COMMITMENTS

_____

_____

_____

_____

Libby gassing up her Tonka Truck

13

THEFT ON THE FAMILY FARM

---

*Don't do what's comfortable,
do what's right.*

— UNKNOWN

(My Son Damon's Motto)

Case in point: A son working for his father was told by his CPA that it made sense from a tax perspective to have the corporation pay for his Long-Term Care Insurance rather than pay it individually. Because it made sense from a tax perspective, the son went ahead acted on the advice. The son had check writing authority, so it wasn't outside of his rights to do so. However, he did not communicate what he was doing with his father and mother, who still owned the farm. What sounded like a good idea to him, appeared more like dishonesty and theft when dad and mom found out what son had been doing. This may seem like a simple misunderstanding, but theft is theft and this situation seriously deteriorated the relationship between father and son.

~~~~~~

In an environment of few formalities and safeguards, theft is more likely to occur.

~~~~~~

Corporate scandals, embezzlement of funds, front-page headlines about theft only happen in large corporations right? It is believed that these large, faceless corporations are the businesses that are most vulnerable to theft. Sadly, theft may actually be more likely to happen on the family farm where there is a higher level of trust and major financial responsibilities are given to fewer people. An environment where there are fewer formalities and structures in place to safeguard the farm's assets, has all of the right, or wrong, ingredients for internal theft.

Tom Grafton, a CPA from Lincoln, Nebraska and expert in the field shares, "There are two keys to keeping your farm from being stolen from. First is to have a system for prevention and second is to have a system for detection."

WHY DO PEOPLE STEAL?

It isn't always the person you see on the street corner that has a menacing look that is most likely to steal from your farm. Often the more likely perpetrator is someone that looks more middle-class, less threatening and possibly even resembles you. To understand the problem of theft, you must first enter the mind of someone that steals. People steal for many reasons; primarily it is justified by the perpetrator because it is 'need' driven. Usually their view is that this is temporary and perpetuated by the reasoning that the money will be returned when they are done "borrowing" it. Unfortunately, the money or assets rarely finds its' way back to the farm.

The second reason people might steal is because they have uncontrolled access to funds or assets. The temptation of having access to money and thinking that no one will know if some is "lost" is simply too much for some people to overcome. Especially when combined with a perceived need or weakened moral resolve, which leads us to the next motive for theft.

People first steal out of need or out of ease.

The third reason people steal is because of personal pressures. They may have a debt that is coming due. They may have an addiction to drugs, alcohol or shopping that they need to satisfy. They may be in an abusive relationship, and they see the money as a way out. It is easy to see that most of us have reasons to want more money in our lives. Understanding this, and realizing that when people are put in stressful situations they are more likely to succumb to temptation, will help wise farm owners see the necessity of safeguards for not only their financial resources but their loved ones as well.

HOW VULNERABLE IS YOUR FARM?

A huge red flag is an organization where only one person handles financial transactions. Having a second person to count money and to make deposits will not only protect the farm from thieves, it also protects the employees from undue enticement and false accusations if at some time the money doesn't add up. Trusting one person to handle the finances in a family farm is a mistake that is sometimes paid for in theft.

Grafton shares that there are four things you can do to prevent theft in the family farm and three major activities to detect theft when it does happen.

Prevention

- Limit physical access to blank check stock and account for all checks utilized
- Limit authorized signature to the bank account
- Limit access to farm debit/credit cards
- Perform background checks on potential hires

Detection

- Produce monthly financial statements and scan for unusual balances
- Review or perform monthly bank reconciliations to assure accurate preparation and validity of reconciling items
- Receive (unopened) bank and credit card statements each month and review for reasonableness, unknown or unusual activities.

Be aware that the reasons that people steal are varied. Be vigilant in knowing your employees and their personal challenges. Talk about the responsibility that it is for each employee to be a steward of the assets that they are charged to look over. Protect them from their own weaknesses by putting in systems of checks and balances that help them to avoid unnecessary temptation.

Don't have your family farm fall victim to the unfortunate event of theft. Prepare your people, put the systems in place to prevent and detect theft and then move forward with confidence.[11]

---

11 A version of "Theft on the Family Farm" is an article from April 2013 Successful Farming® Magazine. ©2013 Meredith Corporation. All rights reserved.

REFLECTIONS

_____

_____

_____

_____

_____

_____

_____

_____

_____

_____

COMMITMENTS

_____

_____

_____

_____

Damon's Report Card

14

THE FAMILY FARM REPORT CARD[12]

It takes as much energy to wish as it does to plan.

—ELEANOR ROOSEVELT

A s a former professor at the University of Nebraska I am well aware of how grades can be a motivation and a measuring stick for performance. One way that I measure the preparation of a family farm for transition is using what I call a "Family Farm Report Card". It gives families a fun and creative way to gauge whether or not they're positioned for success as they develop a succession plan. As the coordinator of family-business programs at the University of Nebraska, I had many opportunities to see families

---

12 A version of "The Family Farm Report Card" is based on an interview I did with Raylene Nickel for a Successful Farming Magazine article September 2012." Successful Farming® Magazine. ©2012 Meredith Corporation. All rights reserved.

positioned for success and some that are set up for heartache.

When it comes to report cards, everyone usually wants A's, but with this particular report card, you want three C's, two D's, and one F. Those letters represent the most critical building blocks to the successful development of a family business succession plan.

The first C is for Contingency Planning. This plan identifies what happens to management and ownership if the unexpected occurs, such as critical illness or premature death. The second C for is for Cash Flow. The senior generation should determine how much cash flow is needed in retirement as well as the source of that income. Discussing these financial needs and expectations with the succeeding generation is critical. The third C stands for Communication. It's important for all family members to communicate their intentions and expectations for the family business. When will the senior generation step back? What are the expectations of the next generation in this process? It's important for people to communicate their desires about what happens with the operation and with individual members of the family.

C — Contingency

C — Cash Flow

C — Communication

D — Decisiveness

D — Determination

F — Family

The first D is for Decisiveness. The succession planning process requires critical decision-making and should only be undertaken when family members are ready to make hard decisions. Families can waste a lot of time, money, and emotional energy in the process if they're not yet ready to make decisions. Entering into the continuity planning process without an attitude of decisiveness can be more detrimental than not starting the process at all.

The second D is for Determination. Succession planning may not be easy and brings potential for hurt feelings between family members. Yet it's better to have the difficult conversations while you're alive than to have an attorney explain things after your death. You have to be determined to do the work required of the process and to understand that it is hard and has lots of roadblocks. It can be a challenge, for instance, to get professionals to collaborate on your behalf, but you have to be determined to get something done.

F is for Family. Preserving the family's relationships and legacy should be the driving force and incentive to undergo the succession planning process. Some of the hardest work required is exploring individuals' intentions and expectations in order to find out which family members sufficiently share the dream to carry the farm or ranch business forward into the future. These will be the people willing to invest personally and to take emotional ownership of the hands on processes undergirding the production activities of a farm or ranch. Thus, the legacy shaped by the family's hard work and lifestyle would be able to continue. Ignoring the planning process as a means of avoiding the potential conflict inherent in this task of determining actual successors is a band-aid approach and will not lead to permanent success for the farm.

Some of the hardest work required is finding out which family members share the dream to carry the farm forward into the future.

When the senior generation is not around to explain its intentions to the family, leaving it to an attorney instead, that's putting family relationships in jeopardy. If you care enough about family relationships and their continuity, you'll be able to face the tough discussions and get the process started.

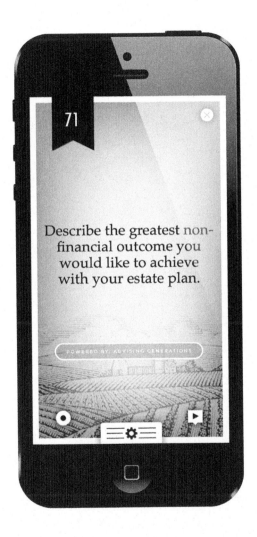

REFLECTIONS

COMMITMENTS

Treasures in Grandpa Wells' Shop

15

YOUR NEW LENS

---

*What you see and what you hear depends a
great deal on where you are standing. It also
depends on what sort of person you are.*

—C.S. LEWIS

Years ago as a young family business consultant I struggled
to get families to execute the technical elements of their
management plan. As I look back the key mistake was
assuming that the controlling owner had all of the power and
influence in executing a continuity plan. What I learned was that
all participants in the family operation needed to be understood
and given some kind of a voice in the process, only then would the
carefully crafted plan move forward with power and impact.

One key tool that helped me to assess the fears, desires and goals of all of these constituents was when I was introduced to a model that focused on the human dynamics of the family business system. Renato Tagiuri and John Davis used a Venn diagram (3 overlapping circles) to help explain the complexities between Family, Ownership and Employment in the family business. This three-circle model can be useful in understanding why people think or feel the way they do about certain issues surrounding the family enterprise.

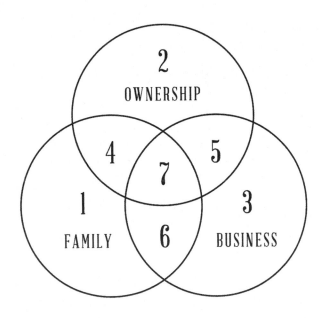

Copyright Tagiuri and Davis

It may be helpful to spend a few minutes defining each group and highlighting some of their unique questions.

1   Family members that neither work on the farm nor have ownership of it.

2   People that have some ownership in the farm but they are not family members and don't actively work on the farm.

3   People who are employees of the farm, but do not have ownership and are not members of the family that owns the farm.

4   Family members who have some ownership of the farm but DO NOT actively work on the farm.

5   People who actively work on the farm and have an ownership stake but are NOT from the family that has the controlling ownership of the farm.

6   Family members and employees of the farm who DO NOT have any ownership in the farm.

7   Family members that actively work on the farm and have some ownership of the farm.

WHAT DO #1S THINK REGARDING THE FAMILY FARM?

This group is made up of family members that neither own the farm or work on the farm. For the most part this group has opinions about the future of the farm, but lack power or influence. This group may feel a sense of nostalgia regarding the farm and may have a general desire to see the farm stay in the family to respect the heritage of their ancestors.

- Why would they change/sell the _____? It was a huge part of our childhood!

- Dad grew hay, Grandpa grew hay, Great-Grandpa grew hay, why would you grow wheat?

- How will I be able to teach my kids about what the farm means to me if I don't own or operate it?

WHO ARE #2S AND WHAT WORRIES THEM?

Typically 2s don't exist in most family farm systems. These owners are neither family members or employees of the farm. This may be an investor or could even be a trustee. This group is very focused on the farm as a financial asset and look at its performance from that standpoint. This group is typically not emotionally invested in the farm, but they do have real questions with how it is being managed and how it is performing.

- What is the farm, or this piece of it, worth?

- How much return am I getting from my investment in the farm?

- This family thinks they want to run it for another generation, but do I trust that they will manage it profitably?

- Would it be better for me to keep this as an investment or sell it?

WHAT DO #3S WORRY ABOUT?

People that would be considered a #3 worry about what will happen to their job if the family that owns the farm doesn't have a plan. They worry about family members returning to the farm and limiting their opportunities or maybe taking their job.

- If Junior comes home from college and wants in does that mean I get the boot?

- Am I always going to be the hired hand?

- How likely is it that the family will keep the farm in the family for another generation?

WHAT DO #4S CARE ABOUT?

Individuals that are family members and have an ownership stake in the farm but do not actively work on the farm have some unique concerns. 4s wonder if they should be patient when the farm isn't providing them with much cash flow. They are sometimes the first to second guess the management of the farm. This group often times feels like they aren't communicated with about what is happening on the farm. While to everyone else it might seem "lucky" to be a non-operating owner of the family farm, it has its own set of challenges.

- Is the farm going to be profitable?

- Should I just wait quietly when the farm is not providing much cash flow?

- Do I view the farm as a community and family stewardship or just a financial asset?

- How do I feel about the management of the farm?

- Do I feel informed about what is really going

on in the farm?

WHAT ARE THE CONCERNS OF A #5?

As a non-family owner and active participant in the farm business, this group has their own set of questions. The group we consider 5s worry about next generation family members coming back to the farm. They sometimes wonder if they are coming back to bring value to the operation or if they are coming back because they couldn't find another job. Wondering about special treatment 5s can also question the compensation of family members that are working in the operation. The biggest worry for this group is that "family issues" begin to creep in and become issues for the farm.

- Are family employees talented and competent?

- Is compensation for family members that work on the farm a fair market wage?

- Does the majority owner have a plan that includes making me an owner with someone I don't want to work with?

- Are family issues, like divorce or sibling rivalry, creeping in and becoming farming issues?

- Do number 4's really understand the long-term value of the strategic plan?

WHAT DO #6S THINK ABOUT?

The perceptions and challenges of a family member that is employed by the family farm without any ownership are distinct. These individuals wonder what it will take to become an owner. They worry about what their parent's will says. They may even fear having to share ownership with all of their non-operating siblings and the challenges that will create. 6s also would like to know if ownership will be gifted to them or if they will need to buy the operation from their parents. Sadly, some wonder if they will be, "just a farm hand" for the rest of their life.

- Does dad/mom have an estate plan that includes me in the ownership of the farm?

- Why does #4 get ownership of the farm when they don't even work on the farm?

- Why does #5 think he/she can boss me around? They aren't even apart of this family!

- Will I ever be trusted to make important decisions?

- What will it take for me to become a #7?

WHAT UNIQUE QUESTIONS DO #7S HAVE?

The unfortunate and sometimes overwhelming challenge of the controlling owner group is that they are forced to deal with all of the questions of all of the other groups. Beyond that, they have a specific set of questions that none of the others face. Many wonder, "Does anyone care about this farm as much as I do?" They also worry about how to satisfy the different needs of each of the other groups. 7s struggle with the questions that surround life after being a controlling owner. Many lack hobbies or other meaningful activities away from the farm. It can be depressing just thinking about having someone else make the day-to-day decisions about the farm that they built. Finally, many struggle to figure out their cash flow needs during retirement. The questions of when to retire, how much money to expect and where it will come from are all typical challenges.

- Does anyone really care about this farm
  or do they just want money from it?

- What would I do if I became anything else but a #7?

- Could I be happy as a #4?

- Do I believe that the next generation is prepared
  to inherit/operate the family farm?

- Do my heirs really understand what I
  had to go through to build this?

- What will I do with my time if I were
  to step away from the farm?

The three circle model isn't just an academic exercise designed to label individuals, it is actually helpful from a practical standpoint so that you can get an idea as to what the individual questions of each participant in the family farm are regarding farm continuity. Take time to go through the exercise of figuring out who fits where in your family farm system and identify the questions and concerns that each group might have. This will not guarantee success, but it will provide a lens through which you can better understand the nuances of the relationships regarding those that have an interest in the farm's future.

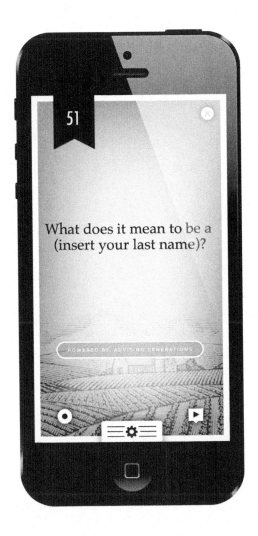

REFLECTIONS

_____

_____

_____

_____

_____

_____

_____

_____

_____

_____

COMMITMENTS

_____

_____

_____

_____

16

CONCLUSION

The path towards generational continuity of your farm operation will require work, but you can do it! It will require communication, but you can do that too! At times it will require individuals in your family to make sacrifices for the betterment of the group or the operation. The ultimate success of your process should be defined first by family relationships being preserved and second by a viable farm business being perpetuated.

There will be times of frustration and moments of uncertainty. The key to realizing your ultimate goal is to remember that this is a process, not an event. Your plans will need to evolve and change as your family and your operation grows. Surround yourself with advisers you trust and peers that can provide context to your succession planning experience.

Ultimately, farm continuity planning is a choice. No one can "make you" put a plan together. You can choose to do nothing or you can choose to do something. Many farmers choose to do nothing for fear of creating conflict or to preserve harmony in the short-term. If that is what you choose, that is okay--if you are comfortable with the plan that the government has laid out for your family operation, doing nothing may be a fine alternative. But if you want to manage the expectations of your family members and control the ultimate ownership and management continuity of your operation, you must thoughtfully engage in this process.

The process should begin with determining the ideal outcome in your mind for the operation and for the family. After you have clarity with your future vision, engage professionals that will translate your desires into a technical plan. Share your thoughts with your family. Ask them for their feedback and then ask them to accept the plan that you create. Finally, review your plans regularly and update them as family and the operation evolves.

The world needs generational farms to succeed. Your community needs your generational farm to succeed. Your family's legacy depends on your choices. Be intentional about the success of your farm. Get started today.

ABOUT THE AUTHORS

Dave and Taneil Specht are the parents of 5 children. Dave is the Founder of Advising Generations, a strategy-consulting firm to family-owned farms, ranches and businesses throughout the United States. He was a lecturer at The University of Nebraska and is best known for his creation of the Inspired Questions—For Farmers mobile app and the Generational Business 360™ process. Taneil is a university-educated woman that has chosen to invest her talents in the home. When she isn't chasing children, she is a writer, proofreader, sounding board and voice of reason in the entrepreneurial process.

THE STORY BEHIND THE PICTURE

1 **Life Lessons From The Tractor Seat:**
This is Grandpa Wells' old Kubota tractor. Taneil grew up driving or walking behind this tractor as her family worked in their apple orchards.

2 **Contingency Plans, Who Needs 'Em:**
This is my oldest daughter Makaley working with some "bummer lambs." She bottle-fed these lambs that either lost or was not accepted by their mother. She learned about life and death and she learned what it meant to have real responsibility. These lambs needed a contingency plan and Makaley was that for them.

3 **I'm Not a Sheep!:**
This is my nephew Rex standing in as actor to replay a scene that happened years ago. In the original scenario Reichert, my son was dressed up by his aunts for our Nativity scene re-enactment at Grandma Wells' house. He thought he was a superhero, not a sheep.

4 **FFA—'Forever Farmers of America', if we aren't careful:**
This is a picture of the FFA leaders from Washington state at the 2015 Convention. This picture was provided by Maya Wahl of Ritzville, WA.

5 **5 Dangers Farmers Should Avoid During the Good Times:**
This is a picture of Jhett and Libby on the family John Deere 790. They are pretty sure they own it.

6 **Enticed or Herded—Farm Continuity Planning:**
This is a picture on branding day 2015 for Van Newkirk Herefords. Kolby and Sara Van Newkirk were students of mine at the University of Nebraska.

7 **10 Things a Farmer Should Never
Say to his Pregnant Wife:**
This is Taneil when she was pregnant with Libby. Jhett had just broken his leg. This woman is amazing!

8 **The Quiet Killer of the Generational Farm:**
This is a picture of me reading Great Grandma Gibbons her favorite Dr. Seuss book. She is 90 and her children all share the responsibility of caring for her. She suffers from dementia, but we have many sweet moments. This was one of them.

9 **Unintended Consequences of Shared Ownership:**
In this picture Libby is taking a swipe at Jhett, her 6 year-old brother. She thinks the tractor is hers and she isn't interested in sharing.

10 **Generational Business 360™:**
This picture was provided by Van Newkirk Herefords in Oshkosh, NE. This is a picture of their neighbor and his children on sale day.

11 **Compensation Conundrum:**
This is Makaley with a handful of fruits and vegetables, an "I Owe You" and a little bit of money. This represents the compensation package of many next generation farmers.

12 **Theft on the Family Farm:**

This is a picture of Libby trying to take some of dad's gasoline to use it in her Tonka truck. "I'm sure dad won't mind."

13 **Family Farm Report Card:**

This is Damon holding a report card behind his back that he isn't too proud of. This isn't real, he's an excellent student, but he's also a pretty good actor.

14 **Your New Lens:**

This magnifying glass was found in Grandpa Wells' shop. This is something he and previous generations use when they are doing detail work on projects.

SPECHT

APPENDIX

A version of, "Life Lessons from the Tractor Seat" appeared in January 2015 Successful Farming® Magazine. © 2015 Meredith Corporation. All rights reserved.

A version of, "Contingency Plans, Who Needs 'Em" first appeared in in Angus Journal in November 2014.

A version of, "I'm Not a Sheep" originally appeared in Nebraska Bankers Magazine in January 2011.

"FFA='Forever Farmhands of America' is an article from August 2015 Successful Farming® Magazine. © 2015 Meredith Corporation. All rights reserved.

"5 Things Farmers Should Avoid During Good Times" is an article from August 2015 Successful Farming® Magazine. © 2015 Meredith Corporation. All rights reserved.

A version of "Enticed or Herded" originally appeared in Nebraska Farmer Magazine in July 2014.

A version of "10 Things a Farmers Should Never Say to His Pregnant Wife" originally appeared on FamilyShare.com in July 2014.

A version of "The Quiet Killer of the Family Farm" is an article from September 2014 Successful Farming® Magazine. © 2014 Meredith Corporation. All rights reserved.

A version of "Unintended Consequences of Shared Ownership" is an an article from December 2013 Successful Farming® Magazine. © 2013 Meredith Corporation. All rights reserved.

A version of "Generational Business 360™" first appeared in The Edge Magazine in May 2012.

CPSIA information can be obtained
at www.ICGtesting.com
Printed in the USA
LVOW04s1328280116
472707LV00027B/624/P